The Drum Beats On

written by Janelle Cherrington
illustrated by Robert Casilla

SCHOLASTIC INC.
New York Toronto London Auckland Sydney
Mexico City New Delhi Hong Kong Buenos Aires

No part of this publication may be reproduced in whole or in part, or stored in a retrieval system, or transmitted in any form or by any means, electronic, mechanical, photocopying, recording, or otherwise, without written permission of the publisher. For information regarding permission, write to Scholastic Inc., Education Group, 555 Broadway, New York, NY 10012.

Developed by Kirchoff/Wohlberg, Inc., in cooperation with Scholastic Inc.

Picture this. It is night. You see a circle and a fire. Cherokee Indians are dancing around it. Their feet move fast.

Rattles are tied around their ankles. The rattles keep the beat with a small drum. The dancers dance all night long. Their feet keep the steady rhythm of the drum.

2

Is this a scene from long ago? Are these ancient Native Americans?

Look closer. You can see hats and jeans. You can see overalls and cowboy boots.

Look at the rattles. Some of the rattles are made out of turtle shells and leather. But some of them are made out of cans.

This is a scene from modern times. This is a Cherokee Stomp Dance!

Stomp dancers dance close to the ground and stomp their feet. They take small, circular steps. They sing songs while they dance.

Some stomp dances are about animals. Some are about friendship. Sometimes they tell a funny story. Sometimes the story they tell is serious.

Today, many Cherokee Indians meet at stomp grounds to dance. They dance to keep the traditions of their ancestors alive.

4

Many Native Americans honor their traditions with dances and songs. Often they do this at festivals called powwows.

Powwows are very popular. There is a powwow almost every weekend in North America. Lots of tribes meet at powwows. Men, women, and children all dance and sing together.

Many kinds of dances are performed at powwows. Some dances are hard. They take years to learn. Others are easy so everyone can join in.

Dancers often dance to songs and drumbeats. Some songs are short. Some have no words. The singers make musical sounds with their voices. Other songs are long. They tell stories, or legends.

Traditional songs and music tell what Native Americans saw long ago.

When the wind blew, it shook the tree leaves. The leaves made noise. This may have given dancers the idea to put rattles on their legs. An eagle's wings moved up and down. This may have given singers the idea to make their arms go up and down.

Native Americans also made instruments long ago. They made rattles out of gourds, horns, turtle shells, and deer hoofs. They made bird-bone whistles and ceramic flutes. They made drums from hollow logs. They made trumpets out of shells.

Native Americans still use these instruments today. They also use metal rattles and bells. They make rattles out of metal saltshakers or cans.

Some powwow dancers add metal fringe to their costumes. The fringe helps them keep the beat as they dance.

Native Americans honor their ancestors in other ways, too. Some make baskets. These baskets have been made the same way for hundreds of years.

Look at these two baskets. Can you tell which one is old and which one is new?

Today's Native Americans make other crafts besides baskets. Some carve wood. Some make jewelry. Some make beautiful pots. Some weave cloth. Some make dolls out of the bark of redwood trees.

Other Native Americans take old ideas from their culture. They use these ideas in new ways. Can you tell which of these totem poles is new? What clue tells you that the totem pole on the left is a new one?

Many Native Americans are proud to share their culture. Many tribes have museums. The Cherokee have one that tells the history of the tribe. It has a village built in the same way as the old villages. Every summer, museum workers put on plays that tell the history of the Cherokee people.

You can visit the museum yourself. It is in the Cherokee Nation in Oklahoma.

Native American traditions gave many things to everyone.

Did you know that the word okay comes from the Choctaw Indians? The Choctaw used it in their meetings. It meant two people agreed.

Did you know that Native Americans invented snowshoes and canoes? Did you know they invented hammocks? Did you know they made the first rubber balls?

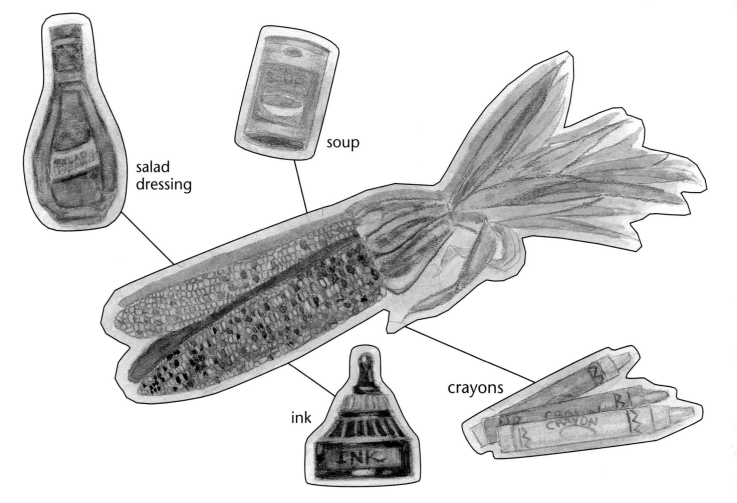

salad dressing

soup

ink

crayons

Native Americans also made the first chocolate. They made the first vanilla. And they found a way to grow corn.

Today, corn is one of the world's most important crops. Cornstarch is made from corn. Cornstarch is in everything from salad dressing to canned soup. It is also in cloth, paper, ink, paint, tape, crayons, toys, roads, and plastics.

15

Native Americans even helped shape the government of the United States. Five Indian nations formed a group called the Iroquois League. All the people in the League were equal. All men, women, and children had a vote.

Benjamin Franklin liked the League's ideas. He used some of them when he helped write the United States Constitution.